An Introduction to Job Applications

Filling in the Blanks

J. Michael Farr
&
Susan Christophersen

from **jist** the job search people

Note: With the recent passage of the Americans With Disabilities Act, citizens with handicaps are now protected from discrimination in hiring. This law has been added to earlier laws protecting against discrimination based on age, sex, race, national origin, religion, and other factors. This is as it should be. Some employers, however, still use older application forms and/or procedures, so we have included some sample questions that are no longer appropriate or, in some cases, legal. We did not do this to offend anyone, nor because we are ignorant of the laws. Instead, we included some items to help prepare job seekers for the reality of the employment screening process as they will find it, and to equip them with a way to deal with the sometimes inappropriate and/or illegal questions they may be asked on applications or in interviews. We are, after all, friends and advocates of job seekers and feel that "being prepared" is better than "being surprised."

Project Director: Spring Dawn Reader
Editor: Sara Adams
Cover Design: Dean Johnson Design Group
Illustration Selection and Arrangement: Mike Kreffel
Interior Design: Spring Dawn Reader
Composition/Layout: Carolyn J. Newland

Career & Life Skills Series: **An Introduction to Job Applications**—*Filling in the Blanks*

©1994, **JIST Works, Inc.,** Indianapolis, IN

99 98 97 96 95 94 93   9 8 7 6 5 4 3 2 1

Send all inquiries to:
JIST Works, Inc.
720 North Park Avenue • Indianapolis, IN 46202-3431
Phone: **(317) 264-3720** • FAX: **(317) 263-3709**

ISBN: 1-56370-090-5

Table of Contents

CHAPTER THREE—How to Use an Application in Your Job Search 59

CHAPTER FOUR—Practice with Applications 71

Introduction

How many times have you started a project, only to find that you don't have the tool you need to complete it? Projects can come to a halt until you get the right-sized wrench, or a smaller paintbrush, or the right measuring cup. Or maybe you've got the right tool, but you don't know how to use it. Anyone can buy a set of tools to tune a piano, for example, but without knowledge and training the tools won't help.

Before you start your job search, you should learn about the tools available to help you. Some of those tools are better than others. Filling out application forms is NOT one of the better tools. (We'll get to why that is later.)

However, most employers require you to fill out an application before they will consider hiring you. So since you have to do it anyway, it's a good idea to learn to make applications work for you, not against you. That's what you'll learn to do in this book.

Applications can be confusing. Many people have problems filling out job applications. Those problems can be avoided by preparation and practice. In this book you will learn about the following:

- Why employers use applications, and what kind of information they want to know

- Problems to avoid when filling out applications

- How to increase your chances of being considered for the job you want

CHAPTER ONE

Application Basics

The goals of this chapter are:

- *To understand why employers use applications.*
- *To learn how applications can be an obstacle to getting a job.*

What Is an Application Form?

An application form provides an employer with information about you. Employers need this information to see if you are the right person for the job they need to fill. The next page shows what an application form looks like. If you want, you can complete it as if you were looking for a job.

Of course, different employers use different forms. This book gives you the general information you'll need and a variety of sample applications for practice.

Bill's

APPLICATION FOR EMPLOYMENT

(PLEASE PRINT REQUESTED INFORMATION IN INK)   Date_____

Bill's is an Equal Opportunity Employer and does not discriminate against any individual in any phase of employment in accordance with the requirements of local, state, and federal law. In addition, Bill's has adopted an Affirmative Action Program with the goals of ensuring equitable representation of qualified women, minorities, Vietnam Era and disabled veterans, and other disabled individuals, at all job levels.

Applicants may be subject to testing for illegal drugs. In addition, applicants for certain positions that receive a conditional offer of employment must pass a medical examination prior to receiving a confirmed offer of employment.

This application will be considered active for 60 days. If you have not been employed within this period and are still interested in employment at Bill's please contact the office where you applied and request that your application be reactivated.

PERSONAL INFORMATION

Last Name	First Name	Middle Name	Social Security No.

Street Address	City	State	Zip Code	County	Telephone No.
					( )

If hired, can you
furnish proof of age?   ☐ Yes   ☐ No

If hired, can you furnish proof that you are legally
entitled to work in the U.S.?   ☐ Yes   ☐ No

Answer the following questions only if the position for which you are applying requires driving.

Are you licensed to drive a car?   ☐ Yes   ☐ No   Is license valid in this state?   ☐ Yes   ☐ No

Have you ever been employed by Bill's or a subsidiary of Bill's?   ☐ Yes   ☐ No

If Yes, note unit number and address	Termination Date	Position

Do you have any relatives employed by Bill's in the store or
unit in which you are applying?   ☐ Yes   ☐ No   If Yes,
Name/Relationship:

In order to assure proper placement of all associates, please list any special skills, training, or experiences which qualify you for the position for which you are applying.

_____

_____

_____

AVAILABILITY

I am applying for the following position:

☐ Sales   ☐ Office   ☐ Mechanical   ☐ Merchandise Handling

☐ Other (specify) _____

Date you are available
to start work: _____

I am seeking (check only one):

☐ Seasonal employment (one season, e.g., Christmas)
☐ Regular employment (employ. for indefinite per. of time)

I am available for:

☐ Part-time employment   ☐ Full-time employment
Complete the Hours Available For Work Chart Below.

If temporary,
indicate dates available:_____

Total hours
available per week:_____

	Mon.	Tues.	Wed.	Thurs.	Fri.	Sat.	Sun.
FROM							
TO							

MISCELLANEOUS

Within the past seven years, have you been convicted of a crime involving dishonesty or violence?
(A conviction record will not necessarily be a bar to employment.)

☐ Yes   ☐ No
If Yes, explain: _____

_____

EDUCATION

Names and Locations of Schools Attended	DID YOU GRADUATE? Yes	No	Course of Study
High School			
College			Major Degree
Other (Name and type)			

WORK EXPERIENCE

List below your four most recent employers, starting with your present or last employer. List under company name any periods of unemployment. If you were employed under another name, please enter under the company name.

Company Name	Address & Phone	Mo./Yr.	Rate of Pay	Title of Job Held / Name of Supervisor	Reason for Leaving
		From	Starting		
		To	Final		
		From	Starting		
		To	Final		
		From	Starting		
		To	Final		
		From	Starting		
		To	Final		

PLEASE READ THE FOLLOWING PARAGRAPH BEFORE SIGNING THIS APPLICATION

I certify that the information contained in this application is correct to the best of my knowledge and understand that any misstatement or omission of information is grounds for dismissal in accordance with Bill's Dependable Co. policy. I authorize the references listed above to give you any and all information concerning my previous employment and any pertinent information they may have, personal or otherwise, and release all parties from all liability for any damages that may result from furnishing same to you. In consideration of my employment, I agree to conform to the rules and regulations of Bill's Dependable Co., and my employment and compensation can be terminated with or without cause, and with or without notice, at any time, at the option of either the Company or myself. I understand that no unit manager or representative of Bill's Dependable Co. other than an Officer of the Company, has any authority to enter into any agreement for employment for any specified period of time, or to make any agreement contrary to the foregoing. In some states, the law requires that Bill's have my written permission before obtaining consumer reports on me, and I hereby authorize Bill's to obtain such reports.

Applicant's Signature_____Date_____

OFFICE USE ONLY

Unit Name and Number			
Employment Date	Dept. or Division No.		☐ REGULAR ☐ PART-TIME
Job Title		Job Code	Job Grade
Compensation Arrangement		Associate No.	Time Card Rack No.
Authorized Signature			Date

Why Employers Use Applications

Imagine that you work for a busy company. You are in charge of hiring new workers. You have three job openings now and about 50 people are applying for each job. You need to fill the jobs as quickly as possible. What's the fastest way to get through 150 job applicants to find the three best ones?

An employer can look through a stack of 150 job applications much faster than he or she can talk to 150 people. In fact, many of those applicants will be ruled out after a quick glance at their applications. This is a process of screening out as many applicants as possible.

Application forms are designed to help an employer quickly spot an applicant's lack of experience or other flaws. An employer does this to eliminate all but the most qualified applicants.

Employers are busy people. They need to fill job openings as quickly as possible. Interviewing a lot of job applicants takes time. But screening out applicants is quick.

The employer's goal is to select workers who:

- can do the job
- will be reliable
- can be trusted
- will work hard

Who Gets Screened Out?

Read the following story to see how an application form can be used to screen you out.

Gary's Story

Gary needed a job. Recently he had seen a sign on the front door of a shoe store. The sign said "Help Wanted." Gary decided to go into the store and fill out a job application.

When he got inside, he spoke with a woman behind the counter. Gary asked her what kind of job they were taking applications for. The woman described the job to Gary. "Can you do a job like that?" she asked.

"I think so," Gary said. The woman handed him an application form. "Please fill out this application form. You can sit down over there," she said, pointing to a chair in a corner. Gary had nothing to write with. He had to ask the woman for a pen.

Another woman sat nearby, also filling out an application. She was wearing a nice dress and good shoes. She looked like she was ready to start working right away, if they wanted her to. She had a notebook next to her and looked at it from time to time while she wrote on the application form.

Gary sat in his chair and looked over the form the woman had given him. There were a lot of small boxes with small printed letters. There wasn't much room to write in the boxes. There were questions Gary didn't understand. Gary had to leave a lot of boxes blank because he didn't have the information the form needed. He didn't know his Social Security number or the address of the high school he had attended. He didn't know the phone numbers of the references the application asked for either. Gary started to fill in the information he knew. He made a mistake, so he had to cross it out. He had to write so small in the space that was left, that it was hard to read.

Gary noticed that the woman sitting nearby was closing her notebook and putting her pen into her purse. She must be finished, he thought. "I'll bet you're glad that's over, huh?" he said, to make conversation.

She looked surprised and then she gave a little shrug. "Oh, it was okay. It's what I expected." She stood up. "It's just another step in the right direction for me," she said. "I'm going to manage this store some day—or another one like it." She smiled. "I know what I want."

As the woman went on her way, Gary looked back over his application. The boxes he had filled in looked messy. By the time Gary handed the form back to the woman at the counter, he felt confused and frustrated.

The woman glanced over Gary's application. "We'll call you if we need you," she said. "Okay, thanks," Gary said. But as he went out the door, he had a feeling that they weren't going to call him at all.

Think About It

• Gary was probably right. This employer is not likely to call him. His application will likely end up being "screened out" as soon as he was out the door.

1. Can you think of some reasons why? Write them in the spaces that follow.

_____

_____

_____

_____

_____

_____

_____

Making a Good Impression

Nearly all large organizations and many small ones will require you to fill out an application form when you apply for a job. You'll have an advantage over most other job applicants if you remember the following principles.

KEY PRINCIPLES TO USING AN APPLICATION
• Use your application to help make a good first impression.
• Avoid answers that can screen you out.

Appearances Count

In order to make hiring decisions, employers often have to rely on their first impressions. They get those impressions from the way you present information about yourself. Employers consider both the information and the way you present it. If employers don't get a good impression from your application, they won't want to interview you. They just won't want to take the time.

Remember the young woman next to Gary who was filling out an application at the same time? Gary noticed that she seemed ready to start working right away. Her appearance made a good first impression on Gary. Her appearance probably impressed the receptionist too. If so, the receptionist might put in a good word to the employer.

First impressions do make a difference. The way you look and the way your application is completed will make a difference. If you make a bad first impression, you may not be considered for the job. This is often true even if you have the skills to do the job. For this reason, you must learn to make a good first impression. This book will help you use your application to make a good first impression.

Hints for Completing Applications

Here are some good practices to follow when filling out applications. Later in this section we will review each one.

- Read and follow all directions carefully.
- Don't leave anything blank. (Write N.A. for "Not Applicable" if something does not apply to you.)
- Look for ways to add positive information about yourself.
- Be as neat as possible.

- Use an erasable black pen.
- Bring names, addresses, dates, and other information you are likely to need with you.
- Avoid giving negative information about yourself.

Example of a Bad Application

On the following pages is a sample application for you to look over. This application has many mistakes. Keeping in mind what you have learned so far, see how many mistakes you can spot. Circle each mistake you find or anything that could be improved on the application.

APPLICATION
FOR EMPLOYMENT

Date _April 1_

BROWN'S IS AN EQUAL OPPORTUNITY EMPLOYER and fully subscribes to the principles of Equal Employment Opportunity. Brown's has adopted an Affirmative Action Program to ensure that all applicants and employees are considered for hire, promotion and job status, without regard to race, color, religion, sex, national origin, age, handicap, or status as a disabled veteran or veteran of the Vietnam Era.

To protect the interests of all concerned, applicants for certain job assignments must pass a physical examination before they are hired.

PLEASE PRINT INFORMATION REQUESTED IN INK.

Note: This application will be considered active for 90 days. If you have not been employed within this period and are still interested in employment at Brown's, please contact the office where you applied and request that your application be reactivated.

Name _Albert C. Smith_   Social Security Number _411 – 76 – 2614_
(Last First Middle)   (Please present your Social Security Card for review.)

Address _1526 N. Otter_
(Number Street City State Zip Code)

County _Marion_   Current phone or nearest phone _____

Previous Address _Same_   Best time of day to contact _any_
(Number Street City State Zip Code)   (Answer only if position for which you are applying requires driving.)

If hired, can you furnish proof of age? ✓ Yes ___ No   Licensed to drive car? ___ Yes ___ No

If hired, can you furnish proof that you are legally entitled to work in U.S.? ✓ Yes ___ No   Is license valid in this state? ___ Yes ___ No

Have you ever been employed by Brown's? Yes___ No ✗ If so, when_____ Position_____

Have you a relative in the employment of Brown's Department store? Yes___ No ✗

A PHYSICAL OR MENTAL DISABILITY WILL NOT CAUSE REJECTION IF IN BROWN'S MEDICAL OPINION YOU ARE ABLE TO SATISFACTORILY PERFORM IN THE POSITION FOR WHICH YOU ARE BEING CONSIDERED. Alternative placement, if available, of an applicant who does not meet the physical standards of the job for which he/she was originally considered is permitted.

Do you have any physical or mental impairment which may limit your ability to perform the job for which you are applying?

Yes, I have a back problem and was in Central State Hospital for 6 months.

If yes, what can reasonable be done to accommodate your limitation?

	School Attended	No. of Years	Name of School	City/State	Grad uate	Course or College Major	Average Grades
EDUCATION	Grammar	6	Holy Trinity	Scranton	yes	General	B
	Jr. High	3	Crestview	"	"	"	B
	Sr. High	3	WCHS	"	"	College Prep	C
	Other						
	College	3	State U	Scranton	NO	Degree	C

	BRANCH OF SERVICE	DATE ENTERED SERVICE	DATE OF DISCHARGE	HIGHEST RANK HELD	SERVICE-RELATED SKILLS AND EXPERIENCE APPLICABLE TO CIVILIAN EMPLOYMENT
MILITARY SERVICE	USA	1985	1988	E-3	radio stuff

What experience or training have you had other than your work experience, military service and education? (Community activities, hobbies, etc.)

I am interested in the type of work I have checked:

Sales ✗   Office ✓   Mechanical ✗   Warehouse ✗   Other (Specify): ✓ _____

Or the following specific Job _anything_

I am seeking (check only one):   I am available for (check only one):

✓ Temporary employment (6 days or less)   ✓ Part-Time

✓ Seasonal employment (one season, e.g. Christmas)   ✓ Full-Time   Work

✓ Regular employment (employment for indifinite period of time)   If part-time, indicate maximum hours per week ___ and enter hours available in block to the right.

If temporary, indicate dates available _____

Have you been convicted during the past seven years of a serious crime involving a person's life or property?

NO ✗   YES   If yes, explain: _drunk in public_

HOURS AVAILABLE FOR WORK	
Sun.	To
Mon.	To
Tues.	To _anytime_
Wed.	To
Thurs.	To
Fri.	To
Sat.	To

REFERENCES

LIST BELOW YOUR FOUR MOST RECENT EMPLOYERS, BEGINNING WITH THE CURRENT OR MOST RECENT ONE. IF YOU HAVE HAD LESS THAN FOUR EMPLOYERS, USE THE REMAINING SPACES FOR PERSONAL REFERENCES IF YOU WERE EMPLOYED UNDER A MAIDEN OR OTHER NAME. PLEASE ENTER THAT NAME IN THE RIGHT HAND MARGIN. IF APPLICABLE, ENTER SERVICE IN THE ARMED FORCES ON THE REVERSE SIDE.

NAMES AND ADDRESSES OF FORMER EMPLOYERS. BEGINNING WITH THE CURRENT OR MOST RECENT	Nature of Employer's Business	Name of your Supervisor	What kind of work did you do?	Starting Date	Starting Pay	Date of Leaving	Pay at Leaving	Why did you leave? Give details
NOTE: State reason for and length of inactivity between present application date and last employer.								
Name J J of Address Walnut St. Tel. No. City Scranton State PA Zip Code	School	Eric Burgess	Clean up	Month ? 90 Year	$6.00 an hr Per Week	Month 3 present Year	$6.00 Per Week	Fired
NOTE: State reason for and length of inactivity between last employer and second last employer. Looked for a job — almost a year								
Name Fred Willis Address ? Tel. No. City Scranton State PA Zip Code	Houses	Rafael	electrician helper labor	Month 8 88 Year	$7 an hr Per Week	Month 10 Year	$7.00 Per Week	boss always picked on me
NOTE: State reason for and length of inactivity between second last employer and third last employer. Looked for a job								
Name Wayne Const. Address 436 N. Anderson Tel. No. 555-4141 City Scranton State PA Zip Code	Construction	Mark Joltz	framing hammer: twisting	Month 6 83 Year	$5.75 Per Week	Month 4 84 Year	$6 Per Week	Company went broke
NOTE: State reason for and length of inactivity between third last employer and fourth last employer. Couldn't find work								
Name Central State Hosp. Address Washington St. Tel. No. City Scranton State PA Zip Code	Mental hospital	Lynn Donovan	Clean up	Month ? 92 Year	$4.20 hr Per Week	Month 7 92 Year	same	I got better and was discharged

I certify that the information in this application is correct to the best of my knowledge and understand that any misstatement or omission of information is grounds for dismissal in accordance with Brown's policy. I authorize the references listed above to give you any and all information concerning my previous employment and any pertinent information they may have, personal or otherwise, and release all parties from all liability for any damage that may result from furnishing same to you. In consideration of my employment, I agree to conform to the rules and regulations of Browns, and my employment and compensation can be terminated with or without cause, and with or without notice, at any time, at the option of either the Company or myself. I understand that no unit manager or representative of Brown's other than the President or Vice-President of the Company, has any authority to enter into any agreement for employment for any specified period of time, or to make any agreement contrary to the foregoing. In some states, the law requires that Brown's have my written permission before obtaining consumer reports on me, and I hereby authorize Brown's to obtain such reports.

Applicant's Signature _Smith, Albert C._

NOT TO BE FILLED OUT BY APPLICANT

INTERVIEWER'S COMMENTS		(Store will enter dates as required.)			Mailed	Completed
I really need a job now	Tested		REFERENCE REQUESTS		not yet	
	Physical examination scheduled for	last year	CONSUMER REPORT			
	Physical examination form completed	I didn't get one	With.Tax (W-4)			
			State With.Tax			

Date of Emp.		
Dept. or Div.	Regular or Part-Time —	
Job Title		
Job Title Code		
Compensation Arrangement	make me an offer	Review Card prepared	Minor's Work Permit
Manager Approving		Timecard prepared	Proof of Birth
Employee No.	Rack No.		Training Material Given to Employee

Prospect for _Albert Smith_

1. ___ 2. ___   Unit Name and Number

An Improved Application

Albert C. Smith's application has many mistakes. How many did you find? It would not make a good impression on any employer. It is messy, includes negative information and has many other problems. The example on the next two pages shows what Albert C. Smith's application should look like when properly filled out.

APPLICATION FOR EMPLOYMENT

Date **April 1, 1994**

BROWN'S IS AN EQUAL OPPORTUNITY EMPLOYER and fully subscribes to the principles of Equal Employment Opportunity. Brown's has adopted an Affirmative Action Program to ensure that all applicants and employees are considered for hire, promotion and job status, without regard to race, color, religion, sex, national origin, age, handicap, or status as a disabled veteran or veteran of the Vietnam Era.

To protect the interests of all concerned, applicants for certain job assignments must pass a physical examination before they are hired.

PLEASE PRINT INFORMATION REQUESTED IN INK.

Note: This application will be considered active for 90 days. If you have not been employed within this period and are still interested in employment at Brown's, please contact the office where you applied and request that your application be reactivated.

Name **Smith   Albert   Claude** Social Security Number **411-76-2614**
　　　　Last　　　　First　　　　Middle　　　　　　　　　　(Please present your Social Security Card for review.)

Address **1526   North Otter Street   Scranton   PA   18602**
　　　　　Number　　　　Street　　　　　　City　　　　　State　　　　Zip Code

County _____

Previous Address _____
　　　　　Number　　　　Street　　　　City　　State　　Zip Code

Current phone or nearest phone **555-1212**

Best time of day to contact **after 12 p.m.**
(Answer only if position for which you are applying requires driving.)

If hired, can you furnish proof of age?　✔ Yes　___ No

If hired, can you furnish proof that you are legally entitled to work in U.S.?　✔ Yes　___ No

Licensed to drive car?　✔ Yes　___ No

Is license valid in this state?　✔ Yes　___ No

Have you ever been employed by Brown's?　Yes ___　No ✔　If so, when _____　Position _____

Have you a relative in the employment of Brown's Department store?　Yes ___　No ✔

A PHYSICAL OR MENTAL DISABILITY WILL NOT CAUSE REJECTION IF IN BROWN'S MEDICAL OPINION YOU ARE ABLE TO SATISFACTORILY PERFORM IN THE POSITION FOR WHICH YOU ARE BEING CONSIDERED. Alternative placement, if available, of an applicant who does not meet the physical standards of the job for which he/she was originally considered is permitted.

Do you have any physical or mental impairment which may limit your ability to perform the job for which you are applying?
No

If yes, what can reasonable be done to accommodate your limitation? _____

EDUCATION

School Attended	No. of Years	Name of School	City/State	Grad uate	Course or College Major	Average Grades
Grammar	6	Holy Trinity	Scranton, PA		General	B
Jr. High	3	Crestview Junior H.S.	Scranton, PA		General	B
Sr. High	3	Warren Central H.S.	Scranton, PA		College Prep	C
Other	—			—		
College	3	Indiana-Purdue University at Indpls	Indpls, IN		Degree Electronics in progress	B

MILITARY SERVICE

BRANCH OF SERVICE	DATE ENTERED SERVICE	DATE OF DISCHARGE	HIGHEST RANK HELD	SERVICE-RELATED SKILLS AND EXPERIENCE APPLICABLE TO CIVILIAN EMPLOYMENT
United States Air Force	6-2-84	4-15-88	A/1C Airman First Class	Radio and small electronics repair

What experience or training have you had other than your work experience, military service and education? (Community activities, hobbies, etc.)

I am interested in the type of work I have checked:

Sales ✔　Office ___　Mechanical ___　Warehouse ___　Other (Specify): **Repair** _____

Or the following specific Job _____

I am seeking (check only one):

___ Temporary employment (6 days or less)

___ Seasonal employment (one season, e.g. Christmas)

✔ Regular emoployment (employment for indifinite period of time)

I am available for (check only one)

___ Part-Time

✔ Full-Time Work

If part-time, indicate maximum hours per week ___ and enter hours available in block to the right.

If temporary, indicate dates available _____

Have you been convicted during the past seven years of a serious crime involving a person's life or property?

NO ✔　YES ___　If yes, explain: _____

HOURS AVAILABLE FOR WORK		
Sun.	8 a.m.	To Close
Mon.	8 a.m.	To Close
Tues.	8 a.m.	To Close
Wed.	8 a.m.	To Close
Thurs.	8 a.m.	To Close
Fri.	8 a.m.	To Close
Sat.	8 a.m.	To Close

REFERENCES

LIST BELOW YOUR FOUR MOST RECENT EMPLOYERS, BEGINNING WITH THE CURRENT OR MOST RECENT ONE. IF YOU HAVE HAD LESS THAN FOUR EMPLOYERS, USE THE REMAINING SPACES FOR PERSONAL REFERENCES IF YOU WERE EMPLOYED UNDER A MAIDEN OR OTHER NAME. PLEASE ENTER THAT NAME IN THE RIGHT HAND MARGIN. IF APPLICABLE, ENTER SERVICE IN THE ARMED FORCES ON THE REVERSE SIDE.

NAMES AND ADDRESSES OF FORMER EMPLOYERS, BEGINNING WITH THE CURRENT OR MOST RECENT	Nature of Employer's Business	Name of your Supervisor	What kind of work did you do?	Starting Date	Starting Pay	Date of Leaving	Pay at Leaving	Why did you leave? Give details
Name Fred Willis Address 1275 E. 11th St. Tel. No. 555-2721 City Scranton State PA Zip Code 18515	Electrical sub-contractor	Rafael Castillo	Electrician Helper	Month 8 Year 89	$280 Per Week	Month Present	$280 Per Week	Work Slowdown - Limited work schedule
NOTE: State reason for and length of inactivity between present application date and last employer. Did odd/independent jobs, college courses - 5 months								
Name Scranton Public Schools Address 593 Walnut Ave. Tel. No. 555-3131 City Scranton State PA Zip Code 18505	Maintenance of school buildings	Eric Burgess	Custodian	Month 7 Year 88	$240 Per Week	Month 3 Year 89	$240 Per Week	Desired a more demanding position.
NOTE: State reason for and length of inactivity between last employer and second last employer. Traveled the United States - 3 months								
Name Grand Forks Air Force Base-USAF Address Hwy 2 Tel. No. 701-597-1111 City Grand Forks N.D. State Zip Code 58211	U.S. Air Force	Technical Sergeant Denise Hagar	Small electronics + radio repair	Month 1 Year 85	$235 Per Week	Month 4 Year 88	$250 Per Week	Term of service expired-Honorable Discharge
NOTE: State reason for and length of inactivity between second last employer and third last employer. Completed basic training + electronics repair school - 6 months								
Name Wayne Construction Address 434 N. Anderson Dr. Tel. No. 555-4141 City Scranton State PA Zip Code 18509	heavy + light constr. wiring	Kim Lenski	Electrical + electronic equip. installer	Month 6 Year 83	$230 Per Week	Month 4 Year 84	$240 Per Week	Company went out of business- Joined U.S. Air Force

I certify that the information in this application is correct to the best of my knowledge and understand that any misstatement or omission of information is grounds for dismissal in accordance with Brown's policy. I authorize the references listed above to give you any and all information concerning my previous employment and any pertinent information they may have, personal or otherwise, and release all parties from all liability for any damage that may result from furnishing same to you. In consideration of my employment, I agree to conform to the rules and regulations of Browns, and my employment and compensation can be terminated with or without cause, and with or without notice, at any time, at the option of either the Company or myself. I understand that no unit manager or representative of Brown's other than the President or Vice-President of the Company, has any authority to enter into any agreement for employment for any specified period of time, or to make any agreement contrary to the foregoing. In some states, the law requires that Brown's have my written permission before obtaining consumer reports on me, and I hereby authorize Brown's to obtain such reports.

Applicant's Signature _Albert C. Smith_

NOT TO BE FILLED OUT BY APPLICANT

(Store will enter dates as required.)

	Tested		Mailed	Completed
REFERENCE REQUESTS	Physical examination scheduled for			
CONSUMER REPORT	Physical examination form completed			
With Tax (W-4)				
State With Tax				

Review Card prepared		Minor's Work Permit	
Timecard prepared		Proof of Birth	
		Training Material Given to Employee	

INTERVIEWER'S COMMENTS	Date of Emp.		
	Dept. or Div.	Regular Part-Time	
	Job Title		
	Job Title Code	Job Grade	
	Compensation Arrangement		
	Manager Approving		
Prospect for	Employee No.	Rack No.	
1.			
2.			

Unit Name and Number _____

Preparation: The Key to Successful Applications

In a different way, Gary had problems in completing his application too. Gary had the skills to do the job. That was not his problem. His problem was that he was not ready to fill out the application. He didn't have the information he needed. He felt confused and frustrated as a result.

You don't have to have the same experience. You can prepare yourself to do a good job on applications. You can make an application work for you instead of against you. This book will help you:

- Learn what to expect from most applications
- Present the best possible impression
- Gather the needed information in advance

☞ Checkpoint

• Answer the questions that follow to review what you have learned in this chapter.

1. Why do employers use application forms?

_____

_____

_____

_____

_____

_____

2. What are four qualities that employers look for in job seekers?

_____

_____

_____

_____

_____

_____

3. Why did Gary have trouble with the job application form at the shoe store?

_____

_____

_____

_____

_____

_____

4. What does it mean to be "screened out?"

_____

_____

_____

_____

_____

_____

⟶ Individual Activity

- Think of a job you might want to apply for. Then look at the four qualities listed below that employers look for in their workers. In the spaces provided, write about how you can show an employer that you have these qualities.

1. I can do the job because

_____

_____

_____

_____

_____

_____

2. I am reliable because

_____

_____

_____

_____

_____

_____

3. I can be trusted because

_____

_____

_____

_____

_____

_____

4. I will work hard because

_____

_____

_____

_____

_____

_____

☞ Group Activity

- Discuss the Albert C. Smith application presented in this chapter. What did Albert do wrong? Did he do anything right? Go through the application section by section with your group and count up all the mistakes. Use the space below to write your own notes.

_____

_____

_____

_____

_____

_____

_____

_____

_____

_____

_____

☞ Alternate Group Activity

- Divide into two or more groups. Each group will look for and count how many things Albert did wrong or needs to improve. The group that finds the most things wrong "wins." Be prepared to explain the mistakes and how each could be corrected or done better. Use the space below to write your own notes.

_____

_____

_____

_____

_____

_____

_____

_____

_____

_____

CHAPTER TWO

Gathering Information for Your Application

The goals of this chapter are:

- *To use more powerful words on your application.*
- *To understand and be able to complete each major section of an application form.*
- *To develop a data base of information to use in answering any question on your application.*

Gathering the Facts

In the first chapter of this book, you learned how employers use applications to help screen people in or out. You also received some general information about how to complete and use an application. Now you will begin to work with actual applications. In this chapter there are worksheets to help you gather the facts you will need to fill out your applications. When you are through completing the worksheets, make copies to take with you when you go to fill out a "real" application and apply for a job.

The Power of Words

The words you use on your application are important. Study the list of action words on the next page. Using these words to describe your work experience can make it more positive. They can help you make a good impression.

Use these or other action words as you fill out the worksheets in this chapter. Action words are very good to use to describe your skills and accomplishments. Action words like these give an employer a very positive impression. They help you tell an employer what you can do.

Action words are important tools to use during your job search. You can use these words on applications and you can also use them in your interviews.

Action Words for Job Applications and Job Search

• Look over the list of action words below. You probably do many of the tasks or use many of the skills that are listed. In your mind, do a quick review of your work experience and education. Then circle every word in the list below that you can use to describe your experience on your applications. This exercise will help you use the power of words to your benefit. Feel free to add your own action words to the list. Then use these and other action words in the worksheets and sample applications throughout this book.

accept	coordinate	handle	report
acquire	counsel	identify	resources
allocate	create	improve	require
analyze	decide	maintain	review
anticipate	define	make	schedule
approve	demonstrate	manage	secure
arrange	design	meet	select
assemble	determine	monitor	ship
assist	develop	organize	select
assume	direct	plan	stimulate
authorize	encourage	prepare	strengthen
change	execute	procure	supervise
compare	exercise	progress	supply
consider	evaluate	promote	teach
contact	furnish	purchase	test
contribute	give	receive	train
control	guide	recommend	upgrade

Dealing with Negative Information

The worksheets that follow will ask you for some information that many applications will not ask. Keep in mind that an application is often used to screen you out. If you give negative details about yourself, it will not help you. Some questions in the worksheets are designed to get information that could get you screened out. The worksheet tips will give you ideas on how to answer these questions in a positive way.

"Illegal" Questions

Laws have been passed to keep employers from using certain information to make a decision about hiring. For this reason, most applications do not ask for information about age, race, religion, national origin, handicaps, or other personal details. In some cases, we ask the information here only to help you plan. For example, do you have a reliable way to get to work? If you have children, have you arranged for good child care? These questions may not be asked on an application but you do need to consider them.

You may also find that some applications **will** ask for this information. In some cases, this information is allowed in order to make hiring decisions about certain jobs. In other cases, the employer may be using out-of-date applications that ask questions that are no longer legal. That is another reason we have included some of these items on the worksheets. These items will have an asterisk (*) sign in front of them.

Telling the Truth

If you feel that answering a question will hurt you, the best thing to do may be to leave that question blank. This is often better than giving details that will get you screened out. Later, during an interview or after you get a job offer, you may tell the employer what you left off the application. But never lie on an application since that can result in your being fired later.

Your Application Data Base

The words "data base" refer to an organized collection of information. In this chapter you will put together a data base of your own. You will use this data base to keep and organize the information you need to fill out applications. Later you can use it to complete an actual job application.

There are many types of application forms. Some are short and simple. Others are long and more complex. Most applications need the same type of information, but there can be differences. The data base you will do in this chapter is very complete. It will help you fill out almost any application.

The worksheets that follow will help you build your data base. Completing each worksheet will help you fill out a section of an application. For example, the personal information worksheet will help you gather the facts about you that many applications need. There are other worksheets for work history, education, and other sections of an application. Each worksheet has tips to help you gather information or complete an application. Remember, items with a asterisk (*), as mentioned in the previous chapter, may be illegal to ask on a real application form.

NEATNESS COUNTS

The neater and more thoroughly you fill out each worksheet, the better prepared you will be to do well on your applications. Make sure each and every entry is as accurate as it can be. Use a pencil or erasable pen on all the worksheets to allow you to make changes.

Data Base----Section I

Personal Information Worksheet

- This worksheet collects personal information about you. Complete each entry as well as you can. Make sure your facts are correct and accurate.

Last Name:_____First Name:_____Middle: _____

Street Address: _____

_____

City:_____State/Province:_____Zip Code: _____

TIP
Include details such as an apartment number on the second address line.

Phone Number: _____

Phone Number for Messages:_____

TIP
If you do not have a phone or answering machine, ask a friend or relative if employers can leave a message with them. You may need to write down more than one number if your phone is not answered during the daytime. That is when most employers will call. Just be sure you make it easy for a potential employer to reach you!

*How long have you lived at your present address? Years:_____Months:_____

Previous Street Address: _____

City:_____State/Province:_____Zip Code: _____

*How long have you lived there?_____

TIP
Few applications will ask these questions but some might. If you have moved many times you may want to write down several addresses.

Social Security Number (or SSN#):_____

TIP
You should have a Social Security card with your name and number on it. This is a nine-digit number assigned to citizens of the United States. It is used by employers to keep track of the taxes and other deductions they send to the government. Everyone gets their own Social Security number. You can get your own number at any age. If you do not have a Social Security card, contact your local Social Security Administration office for details. You can find their phone number and address in the "Blue Pages" of your regular phone directory. Look under "U.S. Government, Health and Human Services Department." *You may have lost your Social Security card or aren't sure if you already have one. If so, explain this to the person at the government office. That person will know how to assist you.*

Are you a citizen of the United States? _____

TIP

Many employers are now required to ask for proof that you are a citizen. If you are not, you may be required to show legal papers that allow you to live and work in this country. Employers can be fined for hiring workers who are not legal citizens.

Position you are applying for: _____

TIP

Many applications say "Position Desired?" This means the same thing. When you fill out an actual application, you may know of a job opening there that you want. If so, write that job title in the space. If not, write down a general title, such as "Office Worker." If you are too specific, the employer may screen you out even if there is another job open in your general area. Whatever you put down, don't say you'll do just "anything."

Schedule of hours desired: _____ a.m./p.m. to _____ a.m./p.m.

Can you work nights? _____ What hours? _____

Can you work weekends? _____ What hours? _____

TIP

Before you fill out an application, have a clear idea of what hours you can work. For example:

- Do you want to work full-time or part-time?
- Do you want a flexible schedule? (changing from week to week)
- Do you want your schedule to always be the same?
- Do you want night-time work, or only day-time hours?
- Can you sometimes work extra hours?

Most people want to work weekdays. If you are willing to work nights or weekends, you may get a job over someone who is not. Many employers will also need you to work some overtime.

---

*How will you get to work? What is your back-up plan, in case your regular transportation fails? _____

_____

_____

_____

TIP

You may not be asked how you will get to work. Some employers just want to know that you can get to work every day on time. Think about how you will get to work. Will you be able to get to work every day, on time? Your answers must convince the employer that you will not miss work due to transportation problems.

Pay or Salary Desired: _____

Note: Some employees get paid on an hourly rate. Others earn a fixed amount per week, or month. How workers get paid depends mostly on the types of jobs they perform.

TIP

An employer wants to know if you are expecting more money than the job pays. This can be a tricky question. Don't write a dollar amount if you can avoid it. It is better to write "open" or "negotiable" instead. This way, an employer will not screen you out based on what you write here.

Find out how much this type of job pays in your area. Later, in the interview, you can mention a pay range such as "five to seven dollars an hour" if the employer asks. That way you won't be eliminated from a job that you may want.

---

*Date of Birth:_____

TIP

It is illegal to discriminate based on age. For this reason, most applications will not ask this question. Child labor laws limit the number of hours and the type of work teenagers are allowed to do and some jobs require you to be 21 years old. An employer can ask your age to make sure they are not breaking a law by hiring you.

The application may ask you if you are over 16 or 21 years of age. If you answer "no," you may be asked to show proof that you are of legal age to work.

*Sex:_____ *Height:_____ *Weight:_____

*Marital Status: _____

TIP
These are also questions that are not often asked on an application. Like any other question, you are not required to answer them. If you are afraid your answers might work against you (screen you out), consider leaving them blank.

*How many dependents do you have? _____

TIP
Dependents are children or other people, including yourself, who depend on you to support them. You claim dependents when you file your tax returns. An employer will need to know this for tax purposes. It is not information often needed on an application before you are hired. Put down "1" if you are claiming only yourself. If you are married, write "2" and continue to add for each child.

Have you ever been bonded [or, can you be bonded?]: _____

TIP
Some employers buy a special insurance for staff who handle money, go into customers' homes, or other situations. The insurance covers any loss to the employer due to theft and certain other losses. If you had ever been bonded, you would know it. Often, the insurance company will check your arrest record before insuring you. So if you aren't familiar with this term, simply answer "no."

*Have you ever been arrested? If yes, give details: _____

_____

_____

TIP

It is legal to ask if you have ever been CONVICTED of a felony (a major crime). Being arrested is not the same as being guilty in this country. Arrests for minor crimes (misdemeanors) do not have to be mentioned at all. Arrests or convictions while you were a juvenile are kept confidential and also do not need to be mentioned. For this reason, few applications will ask you if you have been arrested. Some will ask you if you have been convicted of a felony. If you have not been, say "no." If you have, it may be wise to leave this question blank and bring it up only if you are later offered the job.

---

*Do you have any physical or emotional limitations in doing the job you are applying for? If yes, please describe:_____

_____

_____

TIP

If you can do the job, an employer is not allowed to discriminate based on a handicap. A handicap matters only if it prevents you from doing the work required by that particular job. In most cases, your answer should be "No" or "None that would interfere with my ability to perform the job." If you DO have a disability, you should not consider a job that you cannot do. For example, you may not be able to lift over 20 pounds. Or maybe you get dizzy if you climb a ladder. If so, you should not apply for a job that requires heavy lifting or working at heights where you are not comfortable. As long as you avoid these types of jobs, your limitation or disability is not a problem.

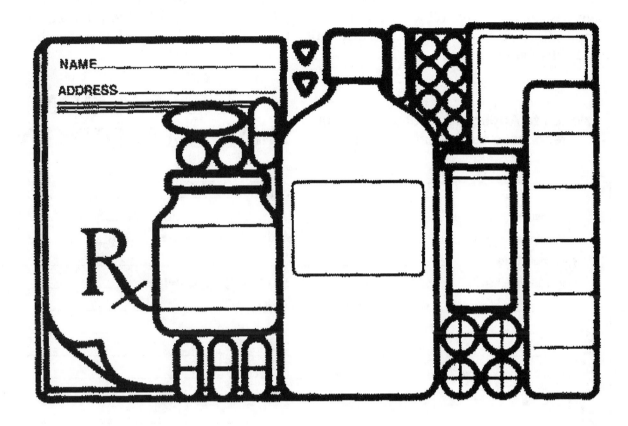

*Have you had any serious illness or injury in the past five years? If yes, please describe:

_____

_____

_____

_____

TIP

Unless you missed more than two weeks of work from an illness or injury, write "no." An application may also ask if you have ever made a worker's compensation claim. An employer wants to know since this will increase their insurance costs. A past illness or injury may also limit your ability to do the job. Or you might miss more work than average if you get ill again.

If you had—or have now—a serious illness or injury, it is best to give as few details as possible. If it is not a problem now, write "None that would interfere with my ability to perform." Or you can simply leave this section blank and explain it before you accept the job. For now, don't let your answer get you screened out in the application stage.

Practice Completing the Personal Section

• Fill out the personal information section of the sample application that follows. Few real applications will be as complete and this one includes information not covered in the worksheets. Remember to follow directions carefully. Employers need to know that you can pay attention and follow directions on the job. So if you are asked to print on the application, be sure to print rather than write. If it asks you to list your last name, then your first name, do it the way it asks. Pay attention to directions!

Notice to Applicants: Please print your responses neatly to all questions

APPLICATION FOR EMPLOYMENT

PERSONAL DATA

Name_____ Social Security No._____

Present Address _____

Telephone Number_____ How Long Have You Lived at Present Address _____

Previous Address_____ How Long? _____

Position Applied for: Work Schedule Desired: ☐ Full-Time   ☐ Part-Time _____

_____ If Part-Time, Specify Hours Desired by Day: Sun _____ _____

_____ Mon._____Wed._____Fri. _____

_____ Tues._____Thurs._____Sat. _____

Rate of pay expected: Start_____6 Mo._____1 Year _____

How did you hear of this opening?_____

_____

Have you worked with us before? ☐ No   ☐ Yes—When/How Long? _____

Previous Job Title_____Reason for Leaving _____

List any friends/relatives working with us now_____

List any special skills you have for positions applied for above _____

☐ Are you over 21? ☐ Yes ☐ No (If No, hire is subject to minimum legal age verification.)

☐ Sex: ☐ Male ☐ Female ☐ Height:_____Ft._____In. ☐ Weight_____lbs.

☐ Marital Status: ☐ Single ☐ Married ☐ Separated ☐ Divorced ☐ Widowed _____

☐ No. Years Married_____No. of Dependents _____

☐ Have you ever been bonded? ☐ No ☐ Yes—When? _____

☐ Have you ever been convicted of a crime in the past 10 years? (Excluding traffic violations) ☐ No ☐ Yes—If Yes, List
     convictions _____

☐ Do you have any physical handicaps preventing you from doing certain types of work? ☐ No ☐ Yes—If Yes,
     describe handicap/limitations _____

☐ Have you had any serious illness in the pat 5 years? ☐ no ☐ yes—If yes, describe_____

     _____

     _____

☐   _____

     _____

Data Base---Section II

Gathering Employment Information

• The following sections illustrate the kinds of questions asked on the employment section of an application. Use the blanks to fill in the information for a job, paid or unpaid, you have had.

Responsibilities: _____

_____

_____

_____

_____

TIP
Use this section to list everything you did on this job. Include skills, accomplishments, results, equipment used, new skills you learned, training you received, people you trained or supervised, and other details. Be sure to include all the positive things you did.

Tools or Equipment You Used: _____

_____

_____

_____

_____

TIP

List any special tools or equipment that you used or learned how to use on this job.

Reason for Leaving: _____

_____

_____

_____

_____

TIP

State the truth, but put it in a positive way. Don't say "The boss was a jerk" or "got fired." It's better to say "Needed a career change" or "they cut staff with less seniority."

Can We Contact This Employer? _____

TIP

Be ready for this question. It may come up. If you had a supervisor who is not likely to give you a good recommendation, give the name of someone at that organization who will. The higher that person's position, the better.

If you provide the previous employer's address and telephone number, the potential employer might contact that organization with or without your agreement. If you know there is someone who won't speak highly of you, direct the new employer to the best possible person to talk to.

Employment Information Worksheet

Use this worksheet to gather information about jobs you've had before. On an actual application, you will usually be asked to list jobs starting with the most recent one. Do the same with this worksheet. List all of your previous work history in your application data base. Include non-paid work as well, such as volunteer positions you have had. Use blank sheets of paper if you have had more work experience than you can fit on this worksheet.

Job #1 (Your Most Recent Job)

Employer's Name:_____

Employer's Street Address: _____

City: _____

State/Province:_____Zip Code: _____

Position/Job Title: _____

Starting Date:_____Ending Date: _____

Beginning Salary:_____Ending Salary: _____

Responsibilities: _____

_____

_____

_____

_____

Tools or Equipment You Used:_____

_____

_____

_____

_____

Reason for Leaving: _____

_____

_____

_____

_____

Can We Contact This Employer?_____

Supervisor's Name: _____

Phone Number:_____

Job #2 (Your Next Most Recent Job)

Employer's Name: _____

Employer's Street Address: _____

City: _____

State/Province: _____Zip Code: _____

Position/Job Title: _____

Starting Date: _____Ending Date: _____

Beginning Salary: _____Ending Salary: _____

Responsibilities: _____

_____

_____

_____

_____

Tools or Equipment You Used: _____

_____

_____

_____

_____

Reason for Leaving: _____

_____

_____

_____

_____

Can We Contact This Employer? _____

Supervisor's Name: _____

Phone Number: _____

Job #3 (Your Next Most Recent Job)

Employer's Name:_____

Employer's Street Address: _____

City: _____

State/Province:_____Zip Code: _____

Position/Job Title: _____

Starting Date:_____Ending Date: _____

Beginning Salary:_____Ending Salary: _____

Responsibilities: _____

_____

_____

_____

_____

Tools or Equipment You Used:_____

_____

_____

_____

_____

Reason for Leaving: _____

_____

_____

_____

_____

Can We Contact This Employer?_____

Supervisor's Name: _____

Phone Number:_____

Job #4 (Next Most Recent Job)

Employer's Name: _____

Employer's Street Address: _____

City: _____

State/Province: _____ Zip Code: _____

Position/Job Title: _____

Starting Date: _____ Ending Date: _____

Beginning Salary: _____ Ending Salary: _____

Responsibilities: _____

_____

_____

_____

_____

Tools or Equipment You Used: _____

_____

_____

_____

_____

Reason for Leaving: _____

_____

_____

_____

_____

Can We Contact This Employer? _____

Supervisor's Name: _____

Phone Number: _____

Practice Completing the Employment Section

• Use this sample portion of an application to practice filling out your previous employment information. Be as complete as you can.

EMPLOYMENT	Please give accurate, complete full-time and part-time employment record. Start with present or most recent employer.

1	Company Name	Telephone ( )
	Address	Employed (State Month and Year) From: To:
	Name of Supervisor	Weekly Pay Start: Last:
	State Job Title and Describe Your Work	Reason for Leaving

2	Company Name	Telephone ( )
	Address	Employed (State Month and Year) From: To:
	Name of Supervisor	Weekly Pay Start: Last:
	State Job Title and Describe Your Work	Reason for Leaving

3	Company Name	Telephone ( )
	Address	Employed (State Month and Year) From: To:
	Name of Supervisor	Weekly Pay Start: Last:
	State Job Title and Describe Your Work	Reason for Leaving

4	Company Name	Telephone ( )
	Address	Employed (State Month and Year) From: To:
	Name of Supervisor	Weekly Pay Start: Last:
	State Job Title and Describe Your Work	Reason for Leaving

5	Company Name	Telephone ( )
	Address	Employed (State Month and Year) From: To:
	Name of Supervisor	Weekly Pay Start: Last:
	State Job Title and Describe Your Work	Reason for Leaving

Data Base---Section III

Education and Training Worksheet

• Your education and training can be very important to an employer. This worksheet will help you collect the details. It includes sections for all the schools you have attended. It also has sections for training. This would include any formal training as well as training you received at home, in a family business, or other places. Be sure to look over this worksheet before you begin writing.

Elementary School

Name of School: _____

Street Address: _____

City: _____

State/Province: _____

Zip Code: _____

Last Grade Completed: _____

Did You Graduate? _____

Junior High/Middle School

Name of School: _____

Street Address:_____

City: _____

State/Province: _____

Zip Code:_____

Last Grade Completed:_____

Did You Graduate? _____

Special Skills, Training, and Honors: _____

_____

_____

_____

In the spaces below, list any special skills, training, awards, activities, clubs, or
organizations from your junior high school years that might interest an employer. _____

_____

_____

_____

High School

Name of School: _____

Street Address:_____

City: _____

State/Province: _____

Zip Code:_____

Last Grade Completed:_____

Did You Graduate? _____

TIP

If you didn't receive a diploma from the high school you attended, but you have received your GED, (General Equivalency Diploma) answer "yes."

Grade Point Average (GPA): _____

Courses _____

List any courses you took that relate to the job you want: _____

_____

_____

_____

_____

_____

Special Skills, Training, and Honors: _____

_____

_____

_____

_____

_____

List any special skills, training, awards, activities, clubs, or organizations from your high school years that might interest an employer. _____

_____

_____

_____

_____

_____

College, Trade, or Technical School

Name of School: _____

Street Address:_____

City: _____

State/Province: _____

Zip Code:_____

Last Grade or Level Completed: _____

Did You Graduate? _____

Degree or Certificate: _____

Grade Point Average (GPA): _____

Major Courses:_____

List any courses you took that relate to the job you want: _____

_____

_____

_____

_____

_____

Special Skills, Training, and Honors: _____

_____

_____

_____

_____

_____

List any special skills, training, awards, activities, clubs, or organizations from your post high school years that might interest an employer: _____

_____

_____

_____

_____

_____

_____

Other Training or Education:_____

_____

_____

_____

_____

_____

☞ Think About It

• List any other training or education you have received. This might include workshops, seminars, formal training on a job, or in the military. Also include things you learned informally. For example, you might have worked summers on your Uncle Ed's farm. There you learned to work on farm equipment and to take care of animals. Think about what you know how to do. You should include it here even if you didn't learn it in school. Don't miss the opportunity to show off your special skills and knowledge!

_____

_____

_____

_____

_____

_____

Practice Completing the Education and Training Section

Fill out the education and training section of the application that follows. It is more complete than most applications, but will give you some good practice that will help you when you fill out a real one.

	School	Name And Location Of School	Course of Study	No. of Years Completed	Did You Graduate	Degree or Diploma
EDUCATION	College				☐ YES ☐ NO	
	High				☐ YES ☐ NO	
	Elementary				☐ YES ☐ NO	
	Other				☐ YES ☐ NO	

AWARDS AND HONORS
(List special certificates, awards, and honors below)

MEMBERSHIP IN PROFESSIONAL OR CIVIC ORGANIZATIONS
(Exclude those which may disclose your race, color, religion or national origin)

Data Base----Section IV

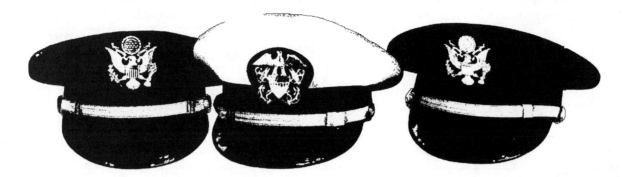

Military Service Worksheet

- Complete this section if you have been in the military. This experience can be as important as any other work experience you've had.

Branch: _____ Rank: _____

Years of Service: _____ From: _____ To: _____

Duties: _____

_____

_____

- In the spaces below list any special duties or responsibilities you had to help describe the type of job or position you had.

_____

_____

Salary:_____

Details of Any Promotions: _____

- Explain in the spaces below any special circumstances of your promotion. For example, perhaps you had outstanding job performances, a superior rating, or took part in a successful training exercise.

_____

_____

Special Skills, Training, and Awards: _____

- List any special education such as schools or courses you attended, training, or skills you acquired during your military service. Be sure to list any awards such as ribbons and medals too.

_____

_____

_____

Practice Completing the Military Service Section

• Use this sample portion of an application to practice filling out your military service information.

MILITARY	BRANCH	ENLISTMENT RANK	HIGHEST RANK HELD	SALARY FROM	TO	REASON FOR CHANGE IN RANK

DESCRIBE DUTIES:

SCHOOLS OR COURSES ATTENDED	LENGTH WEEKS	MONTHS	DID YOU GRADUATE	CERTIFICATE OR DIPLOMA
1.			☐ YES ☐ NO	
2.			☐ YES ☐ NO	
3.			☐ YES ☐ NO	
4.			☐ YES ☐ NO	

LIST ANY SPECIAL SKILLS ACQUIRED DURING YOUR MILITARY SERVICE:

Data Base---Section V

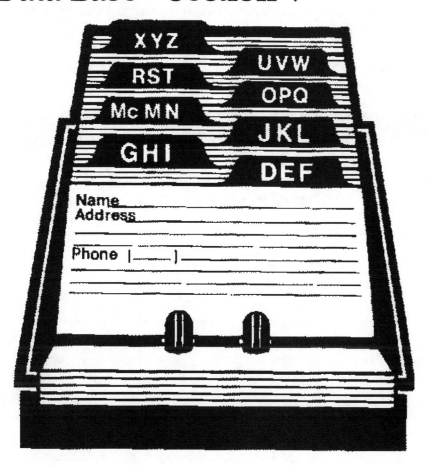

What Is a Reference?

A reference is a person an employer can contact to find out more about you. For example, many employers will want to contact your previous employers. They do this to find out if you are a good worker. Other people who know you well can also be used as a reference. This might include teachers, coaches, or others who know you.

Before listing someone as a reference, be sure that they will say good things about you. The best people to use are those who know that you are a good worker and can be depended on to do a good job. This includes former employers and co-workers.

Former teachers or coaches might make good references. Supervisors from volunteer positions are also helpful. An application for a job might request references both from previous jobs and from personal experiences.

Contact people you know and ask their permission to use them as references. Ask them what they will say about you. It will help to tell them what kind of job you are looking for and the skills you have to do that job. If you feel that they will say good things about you, get their correct mailing address and phone number. Write this in a notebook or piece of paper that won't get lost. This information will be needed on your application.

As you talk to your references, ask them whether they know about any current job openings. They may know of someone who could use a person with your skills. Ask them to keep you in mind if they hear about a job that might interest you. This is called networking and it's one of the most effective job search methods! (You can learn more about networking in another book in this series, *The Two Best Ways To Find A Job*.)

References Worksheet

• List below the people you know from other work experiences or from your personal life who will be able to talk about your skills and abilities that relate to the job you want. Include former school teachers or coaches. Also list people you know who will say good things about you or give you a good recommendation.

Work References

TIP
If you don't have much formal work experience, include names of people who have paid you to do babysitting, lawn-mowing, or other odd jobs. If you have done volunteer work, you can include the name of a supervisor who knows you from this too.

NAME OF REFERENCE: _____

Relationship (How does this person know you?): _____

Name of Organization:_____

Street Address:_____

City: _____

State/Province: _____

Zip Code:_____

Phone Number:_____

What will this person say about you? _____

_____

_____

_____

_____

_____

Did this person give you permission to use them as a reference? _____

TIP
It is good to write down something about yourself that this person could tell your next employer. This way, when you ask them to be your reference, you can also provide them with something good to say. Many times this person will say these things as long as the information is true.

NAME OF REFERENCE: _____

Relationship (How does this person know you?): _____

Name of Organization: _____

Street Address: _____

City: _____

State/Province: _____

Zip Code: _____

Phone Number: _____

What will this person say about you? _____

_____

_____

_____

_____

_____

Did this person give you permission to use them as a reference? _____

NAME OF REFERENCE: _____

Relationship (How does this person know you?): _____

Name of Organization: _____

Street Address: _____

City: _____

State/Province: _____

Zip Code: _____

Phone Number: _____

What will this person say about you? _____

_____

_____

_____

_____

_____

Did this person give you permission to use them as a reference? _____

College, Trade, or Technical School References

TIP
List any teacher or other staff, such as an advisor, who might serve as good reference for you.

NAME OF REFERENCE: _____

Relationship (How does this person know you?): _____

Name of Organization: _____

Street Address: _____

City: _____

State/Province: _____

Zip Code: _____

Phone Number: _____

What will this person say about you? _____

_____

_____

_____

Did this person give you permission to use them as a reference? _____

NAME OF REFERENCE: _____

Relationship (How does this person know you?): _____

Name of Organization: _____

Street Address: _____

City: _____

State/Province: _____

Zip Code: _____

Phone Number: _____

What will this person say about you? _____

_____

_____

_____

Did this person give you permission to use them as a reference? _____

NAME OF REFERENCE: _____

Relationship (How does this person know you?): _____

Name of Organization:_____

Street Address:_____

City: _____

State/Province: _____

Zip Code:_____

Phone Number:_____

What will this person say about you? _____

_____

_____

_____

_____

Did this person give you permission to use them as a reference? _____

High School References

TIP
List any teachers, coaches, or other staff from high school who would give you a good recommendation to an employer.

NAME OF REFERENCE: _____

Relationship (How does this person know you?): _____

Name of Organization:_____

Street Address:_____

City: _____

State/Province: _____

Zip Code:_____

Phone Number:_____

What will this person say about you? _____

_____

_____

_____

_____

Did this person give you permission to use them as a reference? _____

NAME OF REFERENCE: _____

Relationship (How does this person know you?): _____

Name of Organization: _____

Street Address: _____

City: _____

State/Province: _____

Zip Code: _____

Phone Number: _____

What will this person say about you? _____

_____

_____

_____

_____

_____

_____

Did this person give you permission to use them as a reference? _____

NAME OF REFERENCE: _____

Relationship (How does this person know you?): _____

Name of Organization: _____

Street Address: _____

City: _____

State/Province: _____

Zip Code: _____

Phone Number: _____

What will this person say about you? _____

_____

_____

_____

_____

_____

_____

Did this person give you permission to use them as a reference? _____

Personal References

NAME OF REFERENCE: _____

Relationship (How does this person know you?): _____

Name of Organization: _____

Street Address: _____

City: _____

State/Province: _____

Zip Code: _____

Phone Number: _____

What will this person say about you? _____

_____

_____

_____

_____

_____

Did this person give you permission to use them as a reference? _____

NAME OF REFERENCE: _____

Relationship (How does this person know you?): _____

Name of Organization: _____

Street Address: _____

City: _____

State/Province: _____

Zip Code: _____

Phone Number: _____

_____

What will this person say about you? _____

_____

_____

_____

_____

_____

Did this person give you permission to use them as a reference? _____

NAME OF REFERENCE: _____

Relationship (How does this person know you?: _____

Name of Organization: _____

Street Address: _____

City: _____

State/Province: _____

Zip Code: _____

Phone Number: _____

What will this person say about you? _____

_____

_____

_____

_____

_____

Did this person give you permission to use them as a reference? _____

Practice Completing the References Section

• After you collect the data you need, complete the practice application section below. Choose the best references from any category that you listed before.

Personal References (not former employers or relatives)

		NAME AND OCCUPATION	ADDRESS	PHONE NUMBER
REFERENCE CHECK	1.			
	2.			
	3.			

⚐ Checkpoint

• Answer the following questions to review what you have learned in this chapter.

1. Is your data base complete? Go back over it and look for any trouble spots. If you don't know how to find certain information, ask for help. Ask a friend, a librarian, a teacher, or someone else. The more complete your data base, the more confidence you'll have when you do your real applications! List trouble spots or areas where you need to gather more information.

_____

_____

_____

_____

_____

_____

_____

_____

_____

_____

2. Completing your data base can make you more aware of your special skills and strengths. With these in mind, what are some jobs that you might be suited for? List them below.

_____

_____

_____

_____

_____

_____

_____

_____

_____

_____

_____

↠ Individual Activity

1. In the space that follows, describe your perfect job. What type of job would it be? What sorts of things would you do? How would you spend your time?

_____

_____

_____

_____

_____

_____

_____

_____

_____

_____

_____

2. If you were to apply for that job today, would you be qualified? If not, what experience, training, or skills would you need so that you could get that job?

_____

_____

_____

_____

_____

_____

_____

_____

_____

_____

_____

_____

⚐ Group Activity

• Discuss problem areas you found as you completed your data base. (If some of this information is embarrassing to you, you don't have to talk about it.) What are the "traps" that you can fall into on an application? Give each other ideas for handling these traps successfully. Use the space below to write your own notes.

_____

_____

_____

_____

_____

_____

_____

_____

_____

_____

_____

_____

_____

_____

_____

_____

_____

_____

_____

_____

_____

_____

_____

_____

_____

_____

CHAPTER THREE

How to Use an Application in Your Job Search

The goals of this chapter are:

- *To review the major points you have learned in this book.*
- *To learn techniques for using the application in the job search.*
- *To understand how an employer will use an application in the screening process.*

Putting It All Together

In chapter 1, you learned some basic information about applications. You learned what they are and how they are used. You also learned that applications are often used to screen you out. This makes it important to fill out an application in the right way.

In chapter 2, you gathered information and put together your "data base." This data base now includes most of the information you need to fill out an application. You also got some practice in filling out sections of sample application forms. And you learned how to use an application to make a good impression.

Now it's time to learn how to use the application in your job search. Let's begin by doing a quick review of the important points you've learned so far. Take the "quiz" that follows. It won't be graded, so just do your best. Read each question and check whether you think the statement is "true" or "false." When you are done, read the "correct" answers to see how well you did.

Applications Review Quiz

QUESTION	TRUE	FALSE
1. An application is one of the best tools you can use to get a job.		
2. Employers use applications to look for reasons to hire you.		
3. When filling out an application you don't have to be completely honest.		
4. Applications can help you get a job if you know how to do them well.		
5. Applications can keep you from getting a job even if you are well qualified.		

Answers to the Applications Review Quiz

1. **False.** Application forms don't make it easy for you to show off your best qualities. There are many job search tools and methods that are more effective. (You can learn about these methods in other books in this series.) But since many employers use applications, learning to do them well is an important part of your job search.

2. **False.** Employers actually use applications to look for reasons NOT to hire you. A quick glance at your application might make an employer think that you are:

   - too sloppy
   - underqualified
   - unreliable
   - overqualified

   Note: These are just to name a few things. Your task is to make a positive impression. Everyone has flaws. You need to convince an employer that your strengths make up for any weaknesses you might have.

3. **False.** Dishonesty is not a good idea in any part of your job search. An employer can fire you for lying on an application. It is better to leave a section blank if you think the information will hurt your chances of getting hired. You may want to save this information for the interview instead.

4. **True.** An application can help you get a job if it helps make a good first impression. Use it to present your strengths.

5. **True.** Employers often do not hire the best qualified person. Why? Because these people don't always present themselves well. If your application makes a bad impression, you will be screened out right away.

Making Applications Work for You

You have already learned some tips on filling out each section of an application. In general, there are three rules that you can follow in completing an application. Let's explore each one.

Three Rules for Completing an Application

RULE #1: Be As Neat and Complete As Possible

We've covered some of the points under this rule already, but they are worth repeating. Neatness makes a positive impression. Messy applications make a negative one.

Neatness shows that you pay attention to details. It also shows that you are careful with your work, follow directions, and are willing to make the extra effort. These qualities mean a lot to an employer.

Print as neatly as you can. Do not cross out mistakes. Instead, use a black ink pen that erases. This will let you erase mistakes if you make any.

Read and follow all the directions carefully. Fill out each section completely and do not leave blank spaces if you can avoid it.

RULE #2: Be Positive!

A positive attitude will serve you well in every part of your job search. Does being positive mean you should be less than honest? No. It means that you make sure that you include the positive things that you have done or can do. Even if something seems negative, try to include the positive side.

For example, say that you have had several jobs in the past that show no clear direction. This could look negative to an employer. But what if you learned valuable skills on those jobs? Perhaps you learned to get along with many different people and situations. Or maybe you learned how to learn new skills quickly. Can employers appreciate qualities like these?

You bet they can! But you have to tell them about your skills. You have to make employers want to know more about you. That is, make them want to invite you to an interview. (Interviewing skills are covered in another book in this series titled *Why Should I Hire You?*)

RULE #3: Be Creative

It's hard to imagine being creative on an application form. It seems to force your life's experience into a bunch of boxes and lines. But you can do it. The trick is to use every space to your advantage.

Look at each space on an application form as an opportunity to present your skills and abilities. Avoid wasting words and make each word count. Use strong action words like the ones listed in chapter 2. Include positive things about yourself, even if the form does not ask for this kind of information.

Think of how your skills and experience support your present job objective. Make sure that you include these in your application. If you have something important to write but the box is too small or the lines stop, keep writing in blank space. Just indicate how you are continuing the information—draw a small, neat arrow, for example, or write, "Please see back of form for more details."

Gary Tries Again

Do you remember Gary, who you read about at the start of this book? Now we will find out what happened to him. Read his story below. After the story, you'll find a copy of an application Gary filled out. Look at it for examples of how to be creative on your own job applications.

Networking Helps Gary Get Job Leads

Gary still needed a job. But he didn't want another experience like the one at the shoe store. He had left there feeling confused and defeated.

"Was selling shoes really for him?" Gary wondered. He realized that he hadn't thought about that before he applied for the job.

Gary remembered the woman who had been filling out an application that same day. "I'm going to manage this store some day—or another one like it," she had said.

He thought of the way she had smiled when she said, "I know what I want." I know what I want. It was such a simple statement, but it made her seem so strong.

Gary knew he had a lot of thinking to do. But he was beginning to feel excited. This business of finding a job was more than just a way to pay the rent. It was a chance to figure out who he was, what he could be, and where he wanted his life to go. Maybe he wouldn't figure it out all at once. But that was okay. At least now he knew what to do. He needed to figure out what sort of a job he really wanted.

There was no "Help Wanted" sign on the front door of Clark's Furniture Store. But Gary knew there might be a job opening there. He'd been talking to everyone he knew, telling them that he was looking for work. Not just any work. He was looking for a job that required his best skills and knowledge. Gary told everyone he knew what skills he had and what kind of a job he wanted.

A friend of a friend of Gary's mentioned Clark's. The friend told him that Clark's had been growing. They just might need someone to handle the increased business. Even though there might not be an opening now, Gary went there to talk to the owner.

Gary's Application Turns into an Interview

Gary looked good—not too dressy for the place, but not too casual, either. He felt good. He had a notebook full of every kind of information he could possibly need for his application.

Gary went in the store and asked for Mr. Clark. They shook hands as Gary introduced himself. Gary explained that he was interested in working in the furniture business. He said that he was good with people, that he had some sales experience, and was not afraid of hard work. He also explained that he was willing to work evenings and weekends and asked Mr. Clark if he had time to speak about a job opening in his company.

Mr. Clark explained that he was busy now but gave Gary an application form to fill out. It was possible, Mr. Clark said, that he could use a person in the warehouse and that if Gary did well there, he could move into selling or other areas.

Gary took a seat and began carefully filling out the application. His notebook lay open beside him. Halfway through the application, a young woman came into the shop. She wore blue jeans and sandals. "Do you have any job openings here?" Gary heard her ask a salesperson. The man gave her an application to fill out. "Do you have a pen?" she asked.

After a few minutes, she stopped writing. "Are you looking for a job too?" she asked Gary, just to make conversation. He nodded and thought for a minute before he said, "I'm going to own a store like this some day." Then he smiled. "I know what I want," Gary said.

After some time, Mr. Clark returned and looked over Gary's application. "Do you have a few minutes?" he asked. "Of course," Gary answered.

"Let's go into my office and talk a little."

Gary glanced behind him. The young woman was gone. She left her completed application on the table. Then Mr. Clark opened the door of his office, and Gary went in.

Gary's Completed Application

Following is a copy of the application that Gary filled out. While this application could be improved, it is neat, complete, and mentions Gary's skills and accomplishments. Look it over carefully for ideas on filling out your own application.

Clark's Furniture

application for employment

PERSONAL INFORMATION

Date 4-28-94   S.S. No. 104-37-2729

Last Name Williams   First Gary   Middle M.   Age 25

Address 8293 RiverView Dr.   Height 5'11" Weight 175 Date of Birth 3-6-69

City Cleveland

Status   Single ✓   Married___   Widowed___
Divorced___   Separated___

State Ohio   Zip 72917

Date you can start Immediately

Telephone 219-464-3209

Have you ever worked for this company before? No   Location?___   When?___

FORMER EMPLOYERS   (List below last 4 employers, starting with the last one first)

Month & Year	Name and Address of Employer	Salary	Position	Reason for Leaving
From October 92 To Present	Mac's Machinery 219 Stacie Lane, Euclid, OH Supervisor Mac Knife Ph:(219) 825-4317	Start $10 Per hr Finish 18,000 yr.	Start Warehouse Worker Finish Sales+ delivery person	No upward mobility. No openings for me to move in to.
Accomplishments	Promoted to counter sales because of the way I handle customers and solve their problems.			
From June 89 To September 92	Marlin's Fresh Cannery 3171 Lakefront, Cleveland Supervisor Charlie Seashore Ph:(219) 823-7309	Start $8.50 hr. Finish $12.50 hr.	Start Dockworker Finish Cannery Worker	Industry slow-down forced Marlin's to go out of business.
Accomplishments	Because I was dependable and reliable, I moved into a position with more responsibility.			
From August 87 To April 89	Yard Pro Lawn Service 411 Summer St. Cleveland Supervisor Brenda Green Ph:(219) 823-3490	Start $5.00 hr. Finish $6.50 hr.	Start Lawncare worker Finish Lawncare worker	I wanted full-time work and this job was only seasonal and part time.
Accomplishments	I worked at this job while I attended junior college and never missed a day of work or my classes.			

Have you ever been convicted of a Felony?   Yes___   No ✓

In case of an emergency notify: June or Ed Williams   Phone: 219-464-2545

Citizen of U.S.A.?   Yes ✓   No___   If not, do you possess an alien registration card?

If yes, give registration card number:

EDUCATION

	Name & Location of School	Date Grad.	Subjects Studied
High School	Lake High School 44 Boxelder Rd., Cleveland	1987	General Courses
College	Lake Port Junior College Rt. 3, Cleveland		Business
Other			

How Gary Got the Interview

Think about Gary's story earlier in this chapter. He got the interview by asking for it, not by filling out an application. Mr. Clark agreed to see him but also asked him to fill out an application. Gary's completed application helped make a good impression on Mr. Clark.

Remember this in your own job search! Filling out applications might get you an interview, but it is also likely to get you screened out. This is because many other job seekers will have more or better experience than you. Or they have more education or training. Based on your application alone, you will probably be screened out while others will be interviewed—if this is the case.

The one who gets the job is the one who gets the interview, not the one who completes the application. For this reason, it is important to always ask to see the person who would hire or supervise you. If that person asks you to fill out an application before they see you, you will be well prepared.

☞ Checkpoint

• Answer the following questions to review what you have learned in this chapter.

1. What was different about Gary when he went to apply for a job this time?

_____

_____

_____

_____

_____

_____

_____

2. Do you think that the young woman who came in after Gary would be considered for the job? Explain your answer.

_____

_____

_____

_____

_____

_____

_____

3. Why is it important to have a job objective? (This question is important even if you are not actively involved in a job search at this time. Keeping your long-term goals in mind can get you through the tough times, such as training, or taking an entry-level job that's below the level you want to be.)

_____

_____

_____

_____

_____

_____

_____

↪ Individual Activity

• Look over Gary's application as if you were Mr. Clark of Clark's Furniture Store. See it through Mr. Clark's eyes. Would you hire Gary? Why or why not?

_____

_____

_____

_____

_____

_____

_____

_____

_____

_____

↪ Group Activity

• If you are in a group, discuss how Gary presented himself on the application. What strengths has he communicated to you? Is there anything you would change on his application to improve it? Use the space below to write your own notes.

_____

_____

_____

_____

_____

_____

_____

_____

_____

_____

_____

CHAPTER FOUR

Practice with Applications

The goals of this chapter are:

- *To learn to follow directions carefully when filling out applications.*
- *To be able to present your "best" self on the application form.*

Putting Pen to Paper

This chapter includes several real application forms. You should fill out each one as if you were applying for a job. Each application form is different, but many ask for similar information. Since many applications ask different questions, the samples here do ask for information not included in earlier samples.

Read the directions carefully for each application. Do this before you fill it out. Also, make sure that you complete each section neatly and completely. Do your best to complete each application as well as you are able. After you are done, ask someone else to look over your completed application samples and suggest any improvements.

DISTRIBUTED BY
ADS INC.

APPLICATION FOR EMPLOYMENT

NAME_____ SOCIAL SECURITY NO. _____

ADDRESS_____ PHONE _____

ARE YOU OVER THE AGE OF 18? YES ___ NO ___ IF HIRED, CAN YOU FURNISH PROOF OF EMPLOYMENT ELIGIBILITY? YES ___ NO _____

POSITION(S) FOR WHICH YOU ARE APPLYING _____

DATE AVAILABLE FOR EMPLOYMENT _____ IF NOW WORKING, MAY WE CONTACT YOUR EMPLOYER? _____

APPROXIMATELY WHAT SALARY WOULD BE ACCEPTABLE TO YOU IN STARTING A NEW POSITION? _____

HAVE YOU EVER WORKED FOR **ADS, INC.** OR SUBSIDIARY COMPANIES? _____ WHERE? _____ WHEN? _____

DO YOU HAVE ANY PHYSICAL CONDITION WHICH MAY LIMIT YOUR ABILITY TO PERFORM THE JOB(S) APPLIED FOR? YES ____ NO _____

(IF YES, PLEASE EXPLAIN) _____

_____

REFERRED TO **ADS, INC.** OR SUBSIDIARY BY _____

DO YOU HAVE ANY RELATIVES EMPLOYED BY **ADS, INC.**? YES _____ NO _____

NAMES:_____

IN CASE OF EMERGENCY, NOTIFY: NAME _____ PHONE _____

                                ADDRESS _____

HAVE YOU EVER BEEN CONVICTED OF A FELONY? YES _____ NO _____ (IF YES, PLEASE GIVE DATES AND PLACES IN THE U.S.)___

_____

If the job for which you are applying requires that you operate a vehicle, please answer the following:

Do you have a valid vehicle operaor's permit? Yes _____ No _____

By what state was your license issued? _____ Number of auto accidents? _____ Number of tickets _____

EDUCATION

	NAME	LOCATION	NO. OF YRS. ATTENDED	GRADUATED (YES OR NO)	DEGREE OR CERTIFICATE	MAJOR COURSE
HIGH SCHOOL						
BUSINESS SCHOOL						
COLLEGE OR UNIV.						
GRADUATE OR TECHNICAL TRAINING						
OTHER	(Include specialized training received in Military Service)					

It is **ADS** policy to comply with all applicable state and federal laws prohibiting discrimination based on race, age, color, sex, religion, national origin, or other protected classification.

AN EQUAL OPPORTUNITY EMPLOYER

PREVIOUS EMPLOYMENT RECORD

Beginning with present or last employer give complete experience including U.S. military service. Account for all periods of unemployment.

EMPLOYMENT DATES		NAME OF COMPANY AND LAST SUPERVISOR	ADDRESS STREET, CITY AND STATE	POSITION AND DUTIES	SALARY RECEIVED	REASON FOR LEAVING
FROM MO. YR.	TO MO. YR.					

Which job have you most enjoyed?_____Why?_____

Which job have you least enjoyed?_____Why?_____

PROVIDE ANY ADDITIONAL ACCOMPLISHMENTS, INTERESTS, EXPERIENCE, OR REFERENCES THAT MAY BE HELPFUL TO **ADS** IN CONSIDERING YOUR APPLICATION. (Excluding organizations, the name or character of which indicates race, religious creed, color, sex, handicap, or national origin of its members.)_____

IN PROCESSING THIS EMPLOYMENT APPLICATION, INQUIRIES MAY BE MADE WHICH WOULD PROVIDE INFORMATION CONCERNING YOUR EDUCATION, EMPLOYMENT, CHARACTER AND MODE OF LIVING. YOU HAVE THE RIGHT TO REQUEST THAT **ADS** COMPLETELY AND ACCURATELY DISCLOSE TO YOU THE NATURE AND SCOPE OF THESE INQUIRIES. SUCH REQUESTS MUST BE MADE IN WRITING WITHIN 30 DAYS OF YOUR COMPLETION OF THIS APPLICATION.

I HEREBY AUTHORIZE **ADS** TO CONTACT ANY AND ALL OF MY EMPLOYERS, REFERENCES, AND EDUCATIONAL INSTITUTIONS FOR THE PURPOSE OF SECURING EMPLOYMENT REFERENCES AND EDUCATIONAL VERIFICATIONS. I HEREBY RELEASE **ADS** AND ITS EMPLOYEES, AS WELL AS ANY COMPANIES AND INSTITUTIONS YOU MAY CONTACT FROM AND AGAINST ANY LIABILITY IN REQUESTING OR RESPONDING TO SUCH REQUESTS.

I UNDERSTAND THAT ANY MISREPRESENTATIONS, OMISSIONS, OR FALSIFICATIONS OF THE FACTS CALLED FOR ON THIS APPLICATION IS CAUSE FOR DISMISSAL.

I UNDERSTAND THAT NO CONTRACT OF EMPLOYMENT IS BEING OFFERED BY THIS APPLICATION. I FURTHER UNDERSTAND AND AGREE THAT ANY EMPLOYMENT OFFERED IS FOR NO DEFINITE PERIOD AND MAY BE TERMINATED AT ANY TIME WITHOUT PREVIOUS NOTICE.

I UNDERSTAND THAT NO SUPERVISIOR, MANAGER, OR EXECUTIVE OF **ADS**, OTHER THAN THE PRESIDENT, HAS ANY AUTHORITY TO ALTER THE FORGOING.

I CERTIFY THAT I HAVE READ, UNDERSTAND AND AGREE WITH THE STATEMENTS SET FORTH ABOVE.

_____   _____
SIGNED   DATE

Employment Application

DATE_____

SOCIAL SECURITY NO._____

NAME (Print)_____
               LAST   FIRST   MIDDLE   MAIDEN NAME IF MARRIED

BIRTHDATE_____WEIGHT_____HEIGHT_____COLOR EYES_____COLOR HAIR_____
         MONTH   DAY   YEAR

PRESENT ADDRESS_____TELEPHONE NO._____

CITY_____STATE_____ZIP_____

HOW LONG HAVE YOU LIVED AT THE ABOVE ADDRESS?_____U.S. CITIZEN_____TYPE OF VISA_____

IN CASE OF EMERGENCY CALL:

NAME_____ADDRESS_____

RELATIONSHIP_____PHONE NO. (HOME)_____(WORK)_____

MARITAL STATUS: SINGLE_____MARRIED_____WIDOWED_____DIVORCED_____SEP._____ENGAGED_____

SPOUSE'S NAME_____OCCUPATION_____

NO. OF CHILDREN_____AGES_____

FATHER'S NAME_____OCCUPATION_____

PHYSICAL DATA

GENERAL HEALTH: EXCELLENT_____GOOD_____FAIR_____POOR_____

HAVE YOU EVER HAD: TUBERCULOSIS_____HEART TROUBLE_____EPILEPSY_____MENTAL ILLNESS_____

             CHRONIC BACKPAIN_____HEADACHES_____FAINTING OR DIZZY SPELLS_____

DO YOU HAVE ANY PHYSICAL OR HEALTH LIMITATIONS?_____IF YES, EXPLAIN_____

_____

HAVE YOU EVER BEEN TREATED FOR AN EMOTIONAL OR MENTAL DISORDER?_____IF YES, EXPLAIN_____

_____

DO YOU HAVE A CHRONIC AILMENT OR CONGENITAL DISORDER?_____IF YES, EXPLAIN_____

_____

HAVE YOU EVER RECEIVED WORKMAN'S COMPENSATION?_____IF YES, EXPLAIN_____

_____

HOW MANY DAYS OF WORK OR SCHOOL HAVE YOU MISSED IN THE LAST YEAR?_____

EDUCATION

TYPE OF SCHOOL	DATES ATTENDED FROM	TO	SCHOOL NAME AND ADDRESS	MAJOR COURSE	YES	NO	GRADUATE DEGREE
HIGH							
COLLEGE							
BUSINESS							
OTHER							

DESCRIBE ANY EXTRACURRICULAR ACTIVITIES/CLUBS/ORGANIZATIONS YOU PARTICIPATED IN DURING HIGH SCHOOL OR

COLLEGE_____

DO YOU PLAN ANY FUTURE SCHOOLING?_____

JOB DATA

TYPE OF WORK WANTED (1st)_____(2nd) _____

SKILLS/EXPERIENCE RELATED TO JOB WANTED _____

_____

INTERESTS/HOBBIES _____

WORK EXPERIENCE

DATES FROM/TO	NAME & ADDRESS OF EMPLOYER	SUPERVISOR'S NAME	JOB DUTIES	REASON FOR LEAVING

PLEASE ACCOUNT FOR ANY PERIOD OF UNEMPLOYMENT OVER THREE MONTHS IN THE LAST FIVE YEARS._____

_____

_____

MILITARY

BRANCH OF SERV ICE_____DATES OF SERVICE_____TO_____DISCHARGE TYPE_____

SERVI CE RELATED DISABILITY?_____IF YES, EXPLAIN _____

SERVICE RELATED SKILLS _____

HIGHEST RANK HELD_____PRESENT MILITARY STATUS _____

PERSONAL REFERENCES

Do not list relatives, former employers or coworkers

NAME _____	NAME _____	NAME _____
ADDRESS _____	ADDRESS _____	ADDRESS _____
CITY_____	CITY _____	CITY_____
STATE_____ZIP _____	STATE_____ZIP _____	STATE_____ZIP _____
OCCUPATION_____	OCCUPATION _____	OCCUPATION_____
PHONE NO._____	PHONE NO. _____	PHONE NO._____

HAVE YOU EVER BEEN ARRESTED FOR OTHER THAN A MINOR TRAFFIC VIOLATION?_____IF YES, EXPLAIN _____

_____

Personal Qualifications Statement

Read instructions before completing form

1. Kind of position (job) you are filing for (or title and number of announcement	**DO NOT WRITE IN THIS BLOOK** *FOR USE OF EXAMINING OFFICE ONLY*	

2. Options for which you wish to be considered (If listed in the announcement	Material ☐ /Submitted ☐ Returned	Entered register

3. Home phone		4. Work phone			Notations:
Area Code	Number	Area Code	Number	Extension	

5. Sex *(for statistics only)* ☐ Male ☐ Female	6. Other last names ever used.	Form reviewed: Form approved:				

		Option	Grade	Earned Rating	Preference	Aug. Rating
Name *(Last, First, Middle)*						
Street Address or RFD no. *(include apartment no., if any)*					☐ pts. (Tent.)	
City	State	ZIP Code			☐ 10 pts. 30% or more comp. dis	
8. Birthplace *(City & State, or foreign country)*					☐ 10 pts. less than 30% comp. dis	
9. Birth date *(Month, day, year)*	10. Social Security Number				☐ Other 10 points	
11. If you have ever been employed by the Federal Government as a civilian, give your highest grade, classification series, and job title.					☐ disallowed	
Dates of service in highest grade *(Month, day, and year)* From To		Initials and date			☐ Being Investigated	

12. If you currently have an application on file with the Office of Personnel Management for appointment to a Federal position, list, (a) the name of the area office maintaining your application, (b) the position for which you filed, and (if appropriate) (c) the date of your notice of rating, (d) your identification number, and (e) your rating.	**THIS SPACE FOR USE OF APPOINTING OFFICER ONLY** Preference has been verified trhough proof that the separation was under honorable conditions, and other proof as required.

13. Lowest pay or grade you will accept.	14. When will you be available for work? *(month, and year)*	☐ 5-Point	10-Points 30%, or More Compensable ☐ Disability	10-Points less than 30%, Compensable ☐ Disability	10-Point ☐ Other
PAY GRADE $ per OR		Signature and title			
		Agency			Date

15. Are you available for temporary employment :	YES	NO	16. Are you interested in being considered for employment by:	YES	NO
A. Less than 1 month?...............................			A. State and local government agencies?.....................................		
B. 1 to 4 months?......................................			B. Congressional and other public offices?.................................		
C. 5 to 12 months?....................................			C. Public international organizations?.......................................		

(acceptance or refusal of temporary employment will not affect your consideration for other appointments)

17. Where will you accept a job?	YES	NO	18. Indicate your availability for overnight travel:	19. Are you available for part-time positions?	YES	NO
A. In the Washington DC area?			A. Not available for overnight travel...............☐			
B. Outside the 50 United States?			B. 1 to 5 nights per month.............................☐	A. 20 or fewer hours per week?		
C. Anyplace in United States?			C. 6 to 10 nights per month...........................☐	B. 21 ro 31 hours per week?		
D. Only in (specify locality)			D. 11 or more nights per month.....................☐	C. 32 to 39 hours per week?		

20. Veteran Preference. Answer all parts. If a part does not apply to you, answer "No."	YES	NO
A. Have you ever served on active duty in the United States military service? *(Exclude tours of active duty for training in Reserves or National Guard)*...............		
B. Have you ever been discharged from the armed services under other than honorable conditions? You may omit any such discharge changed to honorable or general by a Discharge Review Board or similar authority).. If "YES," you will be required to furnish records to support your claim at the time you are appointed.		
C. Do you claim 5-point preference based on active duty in the armed forces?.. If "YES," you will be required to furnish records to support you claim at the time you are appointed.		
D. Do you claim 10-point preference?... If "YES," check the type of preference claimed and complete and attach Standard Form 15, "Claim for 10-Point Veteran Preference." together with the proof requested in that form		

Type of Preference:	☐ Compensable Disability	☐ Compensable Disab ility Below 30%	☐ Non-compensable Disability	☐ Purple Heart Recipient	☐ Spouse ☐ Widow(er)	o Mother

E. List dates, branch, and serial number of all active service *(enter N/A, if not applicable)*

From	To	Branch of Service	Serial or Service Number

Continued on next page

21. Experience. Begin with current or most recent job or volunteer epxerience and work back. Account for periods of unemployment exceeding three months and your residence address at that time on the last line of the experience blocks in order of occurence.

May inquiry be made of your present employer reegarding your character qualifications, and record of employment　☐ YES　　☐ NO
(A "NO" will not affect your consderation for employment opportunities except for Administrative Law Judge positions.)

A	Name and address of employer's organization *(include ZIP Code, if known)*	Dates employed (give months and year) From　　　　To	Average number of hours per week
		Salary or earnings Beginning $　　　per Ending　$　　　per	Place of employment City State

Exact title of your position	Name of immediate supervisor	Area Code　　Telephone number	Number and kind of employees you supervise
Kind of business or organization (manu-facturing, accounting, social services, etc.)	If Federal service, civilian or military, series, grade or rank, and date of last promotion		Your reason for wanting to leave

Description of work (Describe your specific duties, responsibilities and accompllishments in this job)

For agency use (skill codes, etc.)

B	Name and address of employer's organization *(include ZIP Code, if known)*	Dates employed (give months and year) From　　　　To	Average number of hours per week
		Salary or earnings Beginning $　　　per Ending　$　　　per	Place of employment City State

Exact title of your position	Name of immediate supervisor	Area Code　　Telephone number	Number and kind of employees you supervise
Kind of business or organization (manu-facturing, accounting, social services, etc.)	If Federal service, civilian or military, series, grade or rank, and date of last promotion		Your reason for wanting to leave

Description of work (Describe your specific duties, responsibilities and accompllishments in this job)

For agency use (skill codes, etc.)

C	Name and address of employer's organization *(include ZIP Code, if known)*	Dates employed (give months and year) From　　　　To	Average number of hours per week
		Salary or earnings Beginning $　　　per Ending　$　　　per	Place of employment City State

Exact title of your position	Name of immediate supervisor	Area Code　　Telephone number	Number and kind of employees you supervise
Kind of business or organization (manu-facturing, accounting, social services, etc.)	If Federal service, civilian or military, series, grade or rank, and date of last promotion		Your reason for wanting to leave

Description of work (Describe your specific duties, responsibilities and accompllishments in this job)

For agency use (skill codes, etc.)

22. A. Special qualificatins and skills *(skills with machines, patents or inventions, your most important publication [do not submit copies unless requested]; your public speaking and publications experience, membership in professional or scientific societies, etc.)*

B. Kind of license or certificate *(pilot, registered nurse, lawyer, radio operator, CPA, etc.)*	C. Latest license or certificate		D. Approximate number of words per minute	
	Year	State or other licensing authority	Typing	Shorthand

23. A. Did you graduate from high school or will you graduate within the next nine months, or do you have a GED high school equivalency certificate?

Yes	Month and Year	No	Highest grade completed	B. ame and location *(city and State)* of latest high school attended

C. Name and location *(city, State, ZIP Code, if known)* of college or university. *(If you expect to graduate within nine months give MONTH and YEAR you expect to receive your degree.)*

	Dates Attended		Years Completed		No. of Credits Completed		Type of Degree *(e.g., B.A.)*	Year of Degree
	From	To	Day	Night	Semester Hours	Quarter Hours		

D. Chief undergraduate college subjects	No. of Credits Completed		E. Chief graduate college subjects		No. of Credits Completed	
	Semester Hours	Quarter Hours			Semester Hours	Quarter Hours

F. Major field of study at highest level of college work

G. Other schools or traiing (for example, trade, vocational, Armed Forces or business). Give for each the name and location (city, State, and ZIP Code, if known) of school, dates attended, subjects studied, number of classroom hours of instruction per week, certificate, and any other pertinent data.

24. Honors, awards, and fellowships received

25. Languages other than English. List the languages *(other than English)* in which you are proficient and indicate your level of proficiency by putting an (X) in the appropriate columns. **Candidates for positions requiring conversational ability in a language other than Egnlish may be given an interview conducted solely in that language.** Describe in item 34 how you gained your language skills and the amounf experience you have had *(e.g., completed 72 hours of classroom training, spoke language at home for 18 years, self-taught, etc.)*.

Name of Language(s)	PROFICIENCY							
	Can Prepare and Deliver Lectures		Can Converse		Have Facility to Translate Articles, Technical Materials, etc.		Can Read Articles, Technical Materials, etc., for Own Use	
	Fluently	With Difficulty	Fluently	Passably	Into English	From English	Easily	With Difficulty

26. References: List three persons who are NOT related to you and who have definite knowledge of your qualifications and fitness for the position for which you are applying. Do not repeat names of supervisors listed under item 21, Experience.

Full Name	Present Business or Home Address *(Number, Street, City, State, and ZIP Code)*	Telephone Number *(Include Area Code)*	Business or Occupation

	YES	NO
Answer items 27 through 33 by placing an "X" in the proper column		

27. Are you a citizen of the United States...

    If "NO," give country of which you are a citizen

NOTE: A conviction or a firing does not necessarily mean you cannot be appointed. The circumstances of the occurance(s) and how long ago if (they) occurred are important. Give all the facts so that a decision can be made.

28. Within the last five years have you been fired from any job for any reason?..

29. Within the last five years have you quit a job after being notified you would be fired?..

    If your answer to 28 or 29 is "YES," give details in Item 34. Show the name and address (including ZIP Code) of employer, approximate date, and reasons in each case. This information should agree with your answers in Item 21. Experience.

30. A. Have you ever been convicted, forfeited collateral, or are you now under changes for any felony or any firearms or explosives offense against the law? *(A felony is defined as any offense punishable by imprisonment for a term exceeding one year, but does not include any offense under the laws of a State as a misdemeanor which is punishable by a term of imprisonment of two years or less)*...

    B. During the past seven years, have you been convicted, imprisoned, on probation or parole or forfeited collateral, or are you now under charges fro any offense against the law not included in A above?...

NOTE: When answering A and B above, you may omit (1) traffic fine for which you paid a fine of $50.00 or less, (2) any offense committed before your 18th birthday which was finally adjudicated in a juvenile court or under a youth offender law: (3) any conviction the record of which has been expunged under Federal or State law; and (4) any conviction set aside under the Federal Youth Corrections Act or similar State authority.

31. While in the military service, were you ever convicted by a general court-martial?..
    If your answer to 30A, 30B, or 31 is "YES," give details in Item 34. Show for each offense; (1) date; (2) charge; (3) place; (4) courtt; (5) action taken.

32. Does the United States Government employ in a civilian capacity or as a member of the Armed Forces any relative of yours (by blood or marriage)?....
    If your answer to 32 is "YES," give in Item 34 for such relatives: (1) name, (2) present address (including ZIP Code); (3) relationship, (4) department, agency, or branch of the armed forces.

33. Do you receive, or do you have pending, application for retirement or retainer pay, pension, or other compensation based upon military. Federal Civilian, or District of Columbia Government service?..
    If your answer to 33 is "YES," give details in Item 34. If military retired pay, include the rank at which you retired.

Your Statement cannot be precessed until you have answered all questions, including Items 27 through 33 above.
Be sure you have placed an "X" to the left of every marker above, either in the "YES" or " O" column.

34, Item No.   Space for detailed answers. Indicate Item numbers to which the anwers apply.

If more space is required, use full sheets of paper approximately the same size as this page. Write on each sheet your name, birth date, and announcemnt or position title. Attach all sheets to this Statement at the top of page 3.

ATTENTION—THIS STATEMENT MUST BE SIGNED
Read the following paragraphs carefully before signing this Statement

A false answer to any question in this Statement may be grounds for not employing you, or for dismissing you after you begtin work, and may be punishable by fine or imprisonment (U.S. Code, Title 18, Section 1001). All the information you give will be considered in reviewing your Statement.

AUTHORITY FOR RELEASE OF INFORMATION

I have completed this Statement with the knowledge and understanding that any or all items contained herein may be subject to investigation prescribed by law or Presidenial directive and I consent to the release of information concerning my capacity and fitness by employers, educational institutions, law enforcement agencies, and other individuals and agencies, to duly accredited investigators, Personnel Staffing Specialists, and other authorized employees of the Federal Government for that purpose.

CERTIFICATION	SIGNATURE *(sign in ink)*	Date
I certify that all of the statements made by me are true, complete and correct to the best of my knowledge and belief, and are made in good faith.		

Conclusion

You have learned how an application is often used to screen people out of a job. You have also learned how to create a data base of information and to use it to fill out an application.

But there is more to getting a job than filling out applications. To get a job, you have to know what sort of job you want, what skills you have to do it, and you have to get interviews. Many jobs will also require you to get more education or training.

But many employers will ask you to fill out an application during your job search. For this reason, it is important that you know how to use one to create a positive impression. This and other techniques can help you get interviews. If you make a good first impression in the interview, you then have the chance of being considered for the job you want.

We hope that this book has helped you understand how applications are used in the job search. We wish you well.

More Good Books from JIST Works, Inc.

JIST publishes a variety of books on careers and job search topics. Please consider ordering one or more from your dealer, local bookstore, or directly from JIST.

Orders from Individuals: Please use the form below (or provide the same information) to order additional copies of this or other books listed on this page. You are also welcome to send us your order (please enclose money order, check, or credit card information), or simply call our toll free number at **1-800-648-JIST** or **1-317-264-3720**. Our FAX number is **1-317-264-3709**. **Qualified schools and organizations** may request our catalog and obtain information on quantity discounts (we have over 400 career-related books, videos, and other items).
Our offices are open weekdays 8 a.m. to 5 p.m. local time and our address is:

JIST Works, Inc. • 720 North Park Avenue • Indianapolis, IN 46202-3431

QTY	BOOK TITLE	TOTAL ($)
_____	**Getting the Job You Really Want**, J. Michael Farr • ISBN: 0-942784-15-4 • **$9.95**	_____
_____	**The Very Quick Job Search:** Get a Good Job in Less Time, J. Michael Farr • ISBN: 0-942784-72-3 • **$9.95**	_____
_____	**America's 50 Fastest Growing Jobs:** An Authoritative Information Source • ISBN: 0-942784-61-8 • **$10.95**	_____
_____	**America's Top 300 Jobs:** A Complete Career Handbook (trade version of the Occupational Outlook Handbook • ISBN 0-942784-45-6 • **$17.95**	_____
_____	**The Resume Solution:** How to Write and Use a Resume That Gets Results, David Swanson • ISBN 0-942784-44-8 • **$8.95**	_____
_____	**The Job Doctor:** Good Advice on Getting a Good Job, Phillip Norris, Ed.D. • ISBN 0-942784-43-X • **$5.95**	_____
_____	**The Right Job for You:** An Interactive Career Planning Guide, J. Michael Farr • ISBN 0-942784-73-1 • **$9.95**	_____
_____	**Exploring Careers:** A Young Person's Guide to over 300 Jobs • ISBN 0-942784-27-8 • **$19.95**	_____
_____	**Work in the New Economy:** Careers and Job Seeking into the 21st Century, Robert Wegmann • ISBN 0-942784-19-78 • **$14.95**	_____
_____	**The Career Connection:** Guide to College Majors and Their Related Careers, Dr. Fred Rowe • ISBN 0-942784-82-0 • **$15.95**	_____
_____	**The Career Connection II:** Guide to Technical Majors and Their Related Careers, Dr. Fred Rowe • ISBN 0-942784-83-9 • **$13.95**	_____
_____	**Career Emphasis:** Making Good Decisions • ISBN 0-942784-10-3 • **$6.95**	_____
_____	**Career Emphasis:** Preparing for Work • ISBN 0-942784-11-1 • **$6.95**	_____
_____	**Career Emphasis:** Getting a Good Job and Getting Ahead • ISBN 0-942784-13-8 • **$6.95**	_____
_____	**Career Emphasis:** Understanding Yourself • ISBN 0-942784-12-X • **$6.95**	_____
_____	**Career & Life Skills:** Making Decisions • ISBN 0-942784-57-X • **$6.95**	_____
_____	**Career & Life Skills:** Knowing Yourself • ISBN 0-942784-58-8 • **$6.95**	_____
_____	**Career & Life Skills:** Your Career • ISBN 0-942784-60-X • **$6.95**	_____
_____	**Career & Life Skills:** Career Preparation • ISBN 0-942784-59-6 • **$6.95**	_____
_____	**Living Skills Series:** Effective Communication Skills • ISBN 1-56370-038-7 942784-57-X • **$7.95**	_____
_____	**Living Skills Series** Why Should I Hire You? • ISBN 1-56730-039-5 • **$6.95**	_____
_____	**Living Skills Series:** The Two Best Ways to Find A Job • ISBN 1-56370-040-9 • **$6.95**	_____
_____	**Living Skills Series:** The Skills Advantage • ISBN 1-56370-093-X • **$6.95**	_____
_____	**Living Skills Series:** An Introduction to Job Applications • ISBN 1-56370-090-5 • **$6.95**	_____
_____	**I Am (Already) Successful,** Dennis Hooker • ISBN 0-942784-41-3 • **$6.95**	_____
_____	**I Can Manage Life,** Dennis Hooker • ISBN 0-942784-77-4 • **$8.95**	_____
_____	**Young Person's Guide to Getting and Keeping a Good Job,** J. Michael Farr & Marie Pavlicko • ISBN 0-942784-34-0 • **$6.95**	_____
_____	**Job Savvy,** LaVerne Ludden • ISBN 0-942784-79-0 • **$10.95**	_____

Subtotal _____

Sales Tax _____

Shipping: ($3 for first book, $1 for each additional book.) _____

(Prices subject to change without notice) (U.S. Currency only) **TOTAL ENCLOSED WITH ORDER** _____

___ Check   ___ Money Order   ___ Credit Card: ___ MasterCard   ___ VISA   ___ AMEX

Card # (if applies)_____Exp. Date _____

Name (please print) _____

Name of Organization (if applies) _____

Address _____

City/State/Zip_____

Daytime Telephone (   ) _____ — _____